SARAH ST JOHN

27 Ways to Market and Monetize a Podcast

Copyright © 2022 by Sarah St John

All rights reserved. No part of this publication may be reproduced, stored or transmitted in any form or by any means, electronic, mechanical, photocopying, recording, scanning, or otherwise without written permission from the publisher. It is illegal to copy this book, post it to a website, or distribute it by any other means without permission.

Sarah St John asserts the moral right to be identified as the author of this work.

Sarah St John has no responsibility for the persistence or accuracy of URLs for external or third-party Internet Websites referred to in this publication and does not guarantee that any content on such Websites is, or will remain, accurate or appropriate.

Designations used by companies to distinguish their products are often claimed as trademarks. All brand names and product names used in this book and on its cover are trade names, service marks, trademarks and registered trademarks of their respective owners. The publishers and the book are not associated with any product or vendor mentioned in this book. None of the companies referenced within the book have endorsed the book.

Some links in this book may be affiliate links. This just means that by clicking a link (e-book version) or going to a particular link (print version), that link may be tied to a special link where the author earns a small commission should you buy that particular product, service, or software. This is at no additional charge to the purchaser, and in some cases, may save the purchaser money with special links or coupon codes.

First edition

ISBN: 9798843757366

This book was professionally typeset on Reedsy.
Find out more at reedsy.com

Contents

Preface   v

I   The Basics

Why Podcasting   3
Podcast Host Tips   6
Podcast Guest Tips   9

II   MARKETING A PODCAST

Repurposing A Podcast   15
Social Media Ads   18
Podcast Directory and Listening App Ads   19
How to Get Your Guest to Share Their Episode With Their…   22
Swap, Drop, and Roll   24
Pre-Recorded Masterclass or Interview   26
Virtual Summits   28
Joint Contests   30
Join an Exclusive Membership   31
Dream 100   33
Networking & Referrals   34
Search Over Social   35
Press, Publicity, and Reviews   37

III MONETIZING A PODCAST

Book Funnel	41
6 C's	47
3 M's	49
Sponsorships	51
Affiliate Marketing	53
Pay to Play	55
Skip-The-Line	57
Marketing Boost	58
Guest to Client	59
Conclusion	60
About the Author	62
Also by Sarah St John	64

Preface

This book won't be touching on beginner topics such as what mic to use, how to produce a show, cover art tips, how to determine your niche, etc. There are already several books on this topic. In fact, I wrote one (*Podcastpreneur*) that is available on Amazon. The primary purpose of *this* book is to specifically discuss how to market and monetize a podcast, either as a podcast host and/or as a podcast guest.

If you are looking to expand your knowledge and dive deeper into the topics discussed in this book, be sure to check out these resources:

Get free access to some templates, resources, etc. mentioned in this book by going here:
PodcastProfitPro.com

Need help with your launching, managing, marketing, or monetizing your podcast?
See how we can help!
PodSeam.com

Scan the QR code below to listen to my podcast on your favorite listening device:

I

The Basics

Why Podcasting

Before we discuss why podcasting, let's first talk about what podcasting is. Since you've picked up this book, you are likely already familiar with the concept of podcasting. Nevertheless, here is the definition of podcast according to Dictionary.com: "a digital audio or video file or recording, usually part of a themed series, that can be downloaded from a website to a media player or computer."

So why should you care?

As best-selling author Seth Godin states, "Podcasting is the new blogging." While podcasting has been around since 2004, it's only gained massive traction since 2019.

The number of podcast shows went from approximately 700,000 to 1.5 million during the first few months of COVID-19, with up to 100,000 added each month. At the time of this writing, there are approximately 2.5 million podcasts. Yet only 20 percent of these podcasts are considered active in that they've had an episode published in the past 90 days. Furthermore, there are only about 400,000 podcasts that have more than 10 published episodes. (For the latest statistics, check out MyPodcastReviews.com/stats, which is where I obtained these stats).

While podcasting may seem as if it's getting saturated, keep in mind that there are over 600 million blogs, which means you are 240 times more likely to be found via podcasting than blogging.

Also, podcasting is unlike any other form of content for two big reasons:

1. Aside from audiobooks, podcasting is the only form of content you can consume while multitasking such as commuting to work, washing the dishes, doing the laundry, mowing, and so forth. Since it doesn't involve the eyes the way reading a blog or watching a YouTube video does, it appeals to a much wider audience. People will be more inclined to listen to your full show as opposed to skimming through a blog post or only watching 5-minute videos.
2. Because you can capture someone's attention for longer periods, and also because you are in their ears close to their brain, it won't take long for someone to grow to know, like, and trust you. There's a sense of intimacy involved.

Just like every business needs a website, the day will come when every business should have a podcast. Podcasting is a great front-end funnel method to bring someone into your ecosystem. We'll discuss this further in the monetization section.

Podcasting has gotten me further faster. Imagine that you want to connect with a well-known entrepreneur. You email or call their office and say, "Hey, can I get an hour of your time?" If you aren't flat-out ignored, you will get one of two responses: "No" or "Sure, it'll cost you X for my time," where X is thousands of dollars. Now imagine you have a podcast catering to their target audience. They are much more likely to say yes. Not only will you then get to talk to them, but it'll also be at no charge to you.

I have been able to make connections with and interview people I've looked up to for years. Just having a podcast got my foot in the door. Once you book interviews with well-known people and build up your interview portfolio, then it gives you credibility and authority, which will allow you to book bigger and bigger guests. In addition to the ability to talk with and interview them for an hour—essentially you are getting a free one-hour consultation with them to ask anything you want—you may connect with them beyond just that podcast episode. You may hit it off and form a friendship of sorts. They may hook you up with other thought leaders in your field. The possibilities are endless. Heck, there is even a podcast hosted by Dave Jackson called *Because of My Podcast* where podcasters share stories of the things that have happened as a direct, or sometimes indirect, result of their podcast.

Podcast Host Tips

First and foremost: do research on the guest before the interview. If they have a podcast themselves, listen to an episode or two. Read their blog. Read their books. Check out their social media. Check out their website. Watch their videos. As you do this research, make notes of topics you'd like to discuss in the interview. Don't make a list of specific questions, but create bullet points of general topics and questions. The biggest key is to listen to their answers and form the next question based on their previous answer. Be willing to let the conversation happen naturally. Interject your own thoughts and opinions on topics, especially through telling stories. Contribute to the conversation. This makes for a more interesting and entertaining interview, and it makes you more of an expert to where listeners will continue to tune in to your show for you, not just your guests.

This may sound like stating the obvious, but when reaching out to someone you'd like to have as a guest, make sure they will be appropriate for your show and audience and that they offer value to your listeners. Then set up a scheduling link, otherwise it'll be a bunch of going back and forth.

Tip: When reaching out to big-name guests, it's important to have a one-sheet that breaks down what your podcast is about, the audience demographics, number of monthly downloads, and other stats.

After they book a time, have them fill out a form that asks for their bio, head shot, website, social media links, their CTA or freebie for the listeners, and any other pertinent information.

Two days before the interview, send a reminder email with the date and time of the interview, along with the link for the interview.

Note: I recommend SquadCast over other remote interview options (such as Zoom or Google Meet) as they offer higher-quality audio, record locally, and they don't compress the files.

Two hours before the interview, send that same reminder email with the link for the interview.

After the interview, send a thank-you email with an estimated release date or general time frame for the episode. If the guest has a podcast of their own that you feel you'd be a pleasant guest for, ask them if they'd like to have you as a guest on your show. This is something that can be worked out ahead of time and is referred to as a "pod swap" where you interview each other for each other's shows. It makes the most sense to record these back-to-back while you are at it.

Once the episode is released, send them a link to the episode and any social media graphics you've created for the episode. Let them know you'd appreciate it if they shared it with their social media followers and email list. This is a great way to leverage your guest's audience to grow your own audience. But don't be disappointed if they don't, because the bigger the name, the less likely they are to share it.

After the episode has been released, don't let that be the end of the relationship. Keep the line of communication open, especially if you felt a connection with them, because you never know when you could collaborate again. You may also want to inquire if that guest has any connections where they could do an "introduction" for you. What this means is the guest can vouch for you that it was an enjoyable experience being on your show, and can reach out to the relevant connections they have, encouraging those people to guest on your show. One good way of doing this is to have a list of guests you'd like to have on your show, or vice versa. It can work both ways. You never know who someone you meet may know. With each connection you make, that might open up hundreds of other connections.

It's easy to get guests on your show, but you have to be careful and vet them. You don't want just anyone on your show. Your time is valuable, as is the time of your listeners. Don't just accept everyone that contacts you to be a guest. Make sure their area of expertise applies to your audience. Also, make sure they've been a guest on other podcasts and listen to two of those episodes to get a sense of how well they respond and elaborate on the various questions you might ask. You want guests you can have a conversation with. Guests who don't answer questions with one-word or one-sentence answers are what you want. You want guests who tell stories, give examples, offer advice, and insight. You want guests where you walk away from the interview feeling like you've learned something about yourself. So for these reasons, it's important to listen to episodes they've been on in the past.

There are several services out there that help you find guests or hosts, but I use and recommend PodMatch.

Podcast Guest Tips

Whether you have your own podcast, I would advise to be a guest on other shows. You will gain more exposure by being a guest on other shows than even having your own. If you think podcasting sounds like something valuable you'd be interested in, but you don't want to deal with the scheduling, editing, production, repurposing, etc., then you may not want to start with having your own podcast unless you have the budget to outsource all of those things to a company like mine, PodSeam.com.

But even if you decide having your own podcast isn't your thing, you need to guest on other podcasts. Why? Well, it's a free way (99 percent of the time) to get quick and potentially massive exposure. Say you have a book coming out, or you offer some product or service. If all you had to do was spend an hour per podcast, say you did five podcast guests a month, and each podcast had an audience of just 1,000. That's five hours spent for access to 5,000 super-targeted listeners. Let's say you make sales or get email subscribers from just 10 percent of that. That's 500 paying customers or subscribers (a.k.a. potential future customers). Worth it? Yep.

Let's say you already have your own podcast, so you feel you don't need to also be a podcast guest. The thing is that podcast listeners listen to podcasts. Pretty obvious, eh? So if you are a guest on a podcast, what are the chances those listeners may check out YOUR podcast? Pretty high. You are going to them in their medium of choice. It just makes sense. It's how you grow and scale. And all it costs is your time. So, make a plan to set aside a couple of hours a week to be a podcast guest on other relevant shows. And only go after the shows that are within your niche. Just like it makes little sense to have a guest on who doesn't match your audience, it also makes little sense to be a guest on a show where those listeners aren't your target customer.

It's natural to want to reach for the stars and be on the biggest shows, but you can't start that way. Start out with small shows and build up your guest portfolio before contacting any big podcasts.

With smaller podcasts, it works to just contact them via their website, social media, or email and explain why you think you'd make a delightful guest for their show.

When you approach the big podcasts, you will need to be much more creative, as they potentially receive hundreds of requests weekly. You will need to stand out from the crowd to get past their gatekeepers. One of the best ways to do this is to send a video instead of just a text email. You can do this with a service like Bonjoro or Loom.

Keep the video under a minute. Address them by name, explain who you are, your experience, and why you'd be a pleasant guest for their show. Show how having you on their show is beneficial to *them*, not you. Something I like to do is if they've written a book I've read and enjoyed, I will hold that up and talk about what a brilliant book it is. This proves to them you are a fan or follower of theirs and not just casting your net.

Be sure to listen to at least two episodes before being interviewed so you can get a feel for the flow of the show and what type of questions are asked.

Once you are on the show, be sure to listen to the questions and answer. Whatever you do, don't answer with one-word or one-sentence answers. Hosts like it when you elaborate, share stories and experiences, etc. If you think you are talking too much, you most likely are not. However, it's likely you may not be talking enough. If there are questions, you have for the host, don't be afraid to ask, but I wouldn't recommend asking more than one or two questions. Make sure they apply to the conversation and topic.

After the interview is over, ask them if they know when the episode may go live and tell them you'd love to help them promote it. And then when it goes live, be sure to promote it. A pet peeve of most hosts is when their guests don't even promote the episode they were on, especially if one reason they have guests on the show is to leverage the guest's audience.

I recommend sending a follow-up email later that same day or the next day thanking them for allowing you the opportunity to be a guest on their show. Let them know that you can't wait to hear the episode and share it with your following. I have guest email templates inside Podcast Profit Pro.

When you interview for the show, if you have something coming out that you are promoting on the show such as a book, course, product, etc., see if the host can schedule your episode to release the same week of your launch. If not, it's okay, but it doesn't hurt to at least inquire. One way someone can advance sales is to do a "podcast guesting launch tour." Authors do this when they have a new book coming out. They hit the podcast circuit and do a bunch of interviews leading up to and during their launch. It's a genius way to increase sales.

II

MARKETING A PODCAST

Repurposing A Podcast

You've spent a lot of time recording, editing, and producing your podcast, so it's important to get the most use out of your content. Don't just upload it to your podcast host–stretch that content out by repurposing it. Repurposing is taking a piece of content you created once and then using that same content, or portions of that content, on other mediums.

Foremost, you need to send out your most recent podcast episodes to your email list. For this, I recommend SendFox. You can connect your podcast, blog, or YouTube RSS feeds and links, and it will auto-generate an email showcasing your most recent podcast episodes, blog posts, and YouTube videos.

Some other ways to repurpose a podcast episode are to use a service like Repurpose.io, turn the episode into a long-form audiogram, and upload it to YouTube. Or if you are starting with a video podcast and have that up on YouTube, then turn that video file (MP4) into an audio file (MP3) and upload the audio portion to your podcast host. You can also create short, captioned audiograms for social media. Each platform has its own length requirement. Social channels favor video content over text or photo content. It's also recommended captioning the videos because people may watch it at work or some other place where they can't have the audio up, so they'll read the captions to follow along.

Another type of repurposing is creating graphics and quote cards for social media, particularly Instagram. This is where you take a short, but powerful, quote from your interview guest, or yourself, if it's a solo episode. It's just another form of content in photo form. So you have the video form (audiograms), audio form (the podcast audio), the text form (show notes and transcripts, or both), and now photo form. Include the guest photo on the quote card and their name and then one or two sentences.

Perhaps the most efficient way to repurpose a podcast is to either host a livestream (or record the video and then schedule it to "livestream" using a platform like OneStream Live). With this platform, you can livestream or take an already recorded video and schedule it to "livestream" to YouTube Live, Facebook Live, Instagram Live, Twitter Live, and LinkedIn Live. The reason for livestream is that social media platforms give preference to livestreams. Then you can take that recorded video and upload the full video to YouTube, and create short clips and create YouTube shorts, Facebook stories, Instagram stories, Instagram reels, and TikTok videos. On these, I recommend captioning them so that people can still "watch" these videos without having to have their audio turned on if they are in an environment that isn't conducive to watching with audio. And then strip the audio from the video for your podcast episode. You could also create audiograms and waveforms from the audio, but if you already recorded video (vs audio only), then I'd skip that and just focus on short-form videos instead.

I created the graphic below to give you a visual representation of what I mean on how to repurpose one livestreamed or recorded video into multiple forms of content across multiple platforms.

REPURPOSING A PODCAST

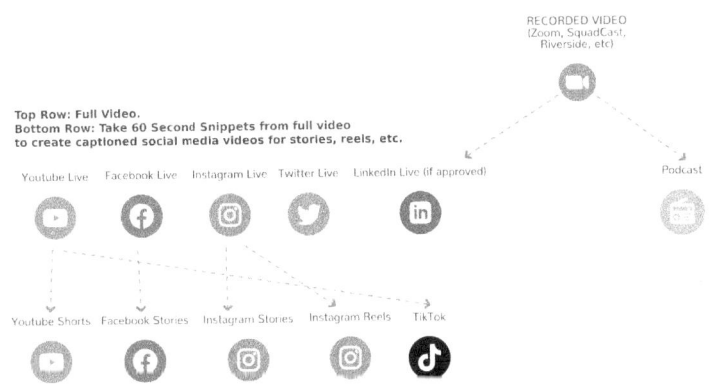

Social Media Ads

I'm just going to start by saying this: social media ads aren't the most ideal avenue to market a podcast because people aren't on social media to find or listen to podcasts. Sure, they could see your ad and still click and listen, but that won't be a high percentage.

However, if you want to test it out, what I would recommend is to promote specific episodes (instead of the podcast) that have guests, you can target their specific audience on social media. The average podcast guest won't be well-known enough to even target their followers, but there may be some guests that you can do this with. If you have guests which you can target their followers, I recommend starting with a $1/day budget per episode.

I would also ensure that you set up different ad sets with specific parameters based on the person's listening device (Apple or Android).

This is a hard subject to describe in written form, so I will be creating a walk-through video in Podcast Profit Pro where I give specific and detailed examples of how to make this work for you.

Podcast Directory and Listening App Ads

Unlike social media ads, you will have a lot more success with podcast directory ads. What this means is your ad will appear in podcast directory or listening apps, usually as a display ad versus a text ad.

First, you know right from the get-go that the person hearing or seeing your ad is already a podcast listener. On social media, you do not know who is or isn't a podcast listener.

Second, since the listener is already in a podcast listening app, there is no barrier to entry. They can just click the ad to check out your show. They won't need to download a new app or be redirected somewhere else.

The only downside to these types of ads is they are much more expensive than social media ads, but with good reason, as I mentioned above.

Here is an example of a more affordable option. This promo was for a $99 one-week ad I did in Castro. The first image is what they tell you can expect from the ad and the second image is how my ad performed.

As you can see, my ad performed better than they promised! That is an ad I would run again because it over-performed and because it's the most affordable paid ad option that I have found.

Some apps let you request a free placement or promo. I have created a list of the various podcast directories and listening apps that either offer free or paid promotions. Where possible, I have also linked to the submission form for each one or directions on how to submit. You can find that list with clickable links to both free and paid promotion or advertising opportunities (as well as screenshots of various ad platform pricing) at PodcastProfitPro.com.

In addition, I will do walk-throughs showing how to set up ads and how they performed with Castro, Buzzsprout, Spotify, PodBay, Disco, and more.

How to Get Your Guest to Share Their Episode With Their Audience

One of the challenging things about having an interview show is just assuming your guests will promote their episode, and then the vast majority of the time, they don't. This is for one or more of the following reasons:

1. They are "too big" or popular of a guest with a large audience already and they don't feel the need to promote the shows they are a guest on.
2. They have already been on many shows and maybe talked about the same things, so they feel if they've promoted one show, they've promoted them all.
3. They don't know how.
4. They are too busy.

There's not much you can do about the first two. However, there is something you can do about the other two.

The first step is to see if you can get a mini-commitment from the guest either before the interview (by mentioning it in your confirmation email) or after the interview (by telling them your post-show process and telling them to expect an email from you with everything they need). Then, once the episode goes live, be sure to do:

1. Email letting them know their episode has gone live and that you'd

appreciate it if they shared it with their audience. Turn it up a notch with a Thank You video (you can create this on Loom or Bonjoro)
2. Make this even easier for them by including assets within the email (or a link to the assets) and this would include any of: audiogram, captioned social media clip, email, or social media script copy they can copy/paste to their emails and social media, an embedded code for them to put on the media/press page of their website, etc.
3. Offer to do an Instagram live with them touching on the topics discussed in the episode with a link to the full video or audio. Tag them on this post.
4. When you share the episode across social media yourself, also be sure to tag them so it alerts them and they can just do a simple "re-share" or "retweet"

I have included email templates for this in Podcast Profit Pro.

Swap, Drop, and Roll

Step 1: Swap It Out

One option to get in front of more listeners is to arrange a pod swap wherein you place a podcast episode from another podcast (relevant to your audience, of course) in your feed for that podcast host placing one of your episodes in their feed. But do this, as your listeners are there to listen to you, not Joe Schmo. But, once in a very blue moon, this can work to both of your advantages.

Step 2: Drop It Like It's Hot

Similar to a full episode swap would be a trailer drop. It would work the same way, except that the swap would just be your trailer (which lasts around 2 minutes).

Another option to get in front of more listeners is to offer to do a feed drop. There are a few ways to do this. One option is if your guest also has their podcast, you could provide the audio file to your guest and have them include it in their feed. Likewise, if you are a guest on another show and you feel it was a good interview, you could ask for the audio file to drop that episode in your feed. I wouldn't recommend doing this very often though, as your audience is there to listen to you and your show. But one or two would be fine, especially if you cover information you never have before on your show.

I did this with a podcast I was a guest on. I thought the interview went well, and we covered topics I hadn't covered in other podcasts, including my own. So I asked for the audio file to drop in my feed. Note: when doing this, be sure to record and include a brief intro explaining what you are doing and why so that the listeners aren't confused or upset.

Another way of doing this is if both of you have podcasts that are within the same niche, you could do a "part one" on one show and a "part two" on the other show. You would then say "To listen to part two of this podcast, be sure to check out the such-and-such podcast". This is also something I would do sparingly, as it may irritate your audience to switch to a new podcast to listen to the second part of or finish an interview.

Step 3: Roll With It

Perhaps the most advisable of all these options is to offer to do an intro or outro swap (or pre-roll or post-roll) with another podcast in your niche. Typically, this would be a free method of getting in front of new listeners because you are exchanging value. However, you could also offer to pay a fee to have a pre, mid, or post-roll placed in another relevant podcast if they aren't wanting to do a swap.

The two places I recommend for either paid promo or intro/outro swaps are:

- Audry
- Buzzsprout Ads

I will be doing an overview of both of these in Podcast Profit Pro.

Pre-Recorded Masterclass or Interview

A problem some podcast guests have is time. As a guest, you'd love to get on as many shows as possible, but that just isn't workable. An option I have presented to some clients is to consider recording an audio presentation and reaching out to relevant podcasts and see if the host would consider your already pre-recorded audio.

Now, this isn't common practice as yet, and it may never be. You will get more no's than yes's because one of the big reasons for having a podcast is for interview communications. However, just like podcast guests are short on time, so are podcast hosts. There may be some hosts in your industry that are short on time and low on podcast episodes "in the tank". This would be a viable option for them to have a masterclass presentation by a "guest host" or "guest speaker". I would recommend the guest and/or host personalize the intro/outro to each podcast episode like this.

If the podcast host declines your offer to provide valuable content to their audience for very little work on their end, you may offer the podcast host compensation for being able to use their platform and leverage their audience. They are more likely to agree to an arrangement like this if there is monetary compensation or some other publicity trade such as a masterclass pod swap where you each record a masterclass that is featured on each other's podcasts.

Another option is to use a service like Rumble Studio where you can record asynchronously. Here you can record your questions, and then have podcast guests record their answers, and then you or your team can splice it all together into a cohesive episode. This avoids the need to find a mutual time to schedule, and reschedule, and oh wait... yes, reschedule once again.

Virtual Summits

A virtual summit is when you gather up a bunch of thought leaders in a relevant field and do an interview with each of these guests. But, instead of including them in your podcast, you would create a summit where all the interviews and content are available at once, and usually in video form. You can either offer this as a low-ticket paid offer, or the more common option is to allow free registration with limited-time replay, and then the attendee would need to pay a certain amount (usually $17 - $297) to have extended or permanent access to the videos, and perhaps some bonus content that wasn't available in the free version.

Aside from the possibility of generating revenue using this method, you also will get in front of a vast audience. To do this, you would sign up each guest as an affiliate so that they earn a portion of sales for anyone they refer from their list who upgrades to the paid version of the summit. In exchange, the guests will email their list (and perhaps post on social media) talking about how they are a guest on the such-and-such summit and encourage their audience to check it out. When one of their email list subscribers signs up for the summit, you now have their email address and are growing your email list. In exchange, the guest may earn a commission if anyone on their email list who clicks their affiliate link to register ends up taking the upsell.

It's a win-win.

I will be including a spreadsheet to keep track of your virtual summit reach outs in Podcast Profit Pro.

Joint Contests

A joint contest is when a guest offers something up to your audience, usually at no charge to you. They will promote the offer to their audience because their audience may end up winning this product or service, but when the subscriber enters their email to enter the contest, you are growing your email list. You would also alert your email list of the contest, which puts the guest's product or service in front of your audience.

I did this with Travis Brown and his PodDecks. He was a guest on my show, and he sent me two free stacks of his complete PodDecks: one to keep for myself and the other to offer for free as a contest. So when he was a guest on the show, we mentioned the contest, and we also both emailed our respective email lists about the contest. I grew my email list, and he got publicity and some new buyers as well.

Also, a win-win.

Join an Exclusive Membership

This is an unconventional method for getting big-name guests, and I can't guarantee this will work for everyone. But, if you want someone on your podcast, but you are finding it difficult to get a hold of them or through their gatekeepers through email, contact form, support tickets, social media, etc, see if they have a paid membership of some sort.

So, let me tell you about my experience with this.

I had tried several times to get Pat Flynn on my podcast, to no avail. When he launched his SPI Pro membership (Smart Passive Income), I figured it was worth checking out. I had no intention of using it as leverage to get him on the show. Once I was a member and logged in to this platform, he uses for this membership; I noticed I could direct-message people, including Pat! So, I messaged him, explaining about my podcast and asking if he'd like to be a guest on the show, and included a scheduling link. Within two hours, he had booked in and messaged me back, saying he'd love to be on the show. Did I think this would work? Not really. I put little thought into it. I just figured it was worth trying.

What this taught me is that sometimes you have to invest a little time or money and/or go where that person is spending time. I doubt he ever saw any of my email requests to have him on the show. I'm sure it went to some general mailbox with a gatekeeper. But, by joining his exclusive membership community, I now had direct access to him.

Again, this won't always work. Maybe I got lucky. But I am of the mindset that a celebrity, entrepreneur, or influencer is more likely to consider your request for an interview if you are paying them and/or involved in their community.

Dream 100

Dream 100 is a concept started by Chet Holmes, but made famous by Russell Brunson, Dana Derricks, Joe Fier, and Matt Wolfe. It is essential when you have a list of your Dream 100 (or whatever number you choose) collaborations, customers, or clients. It's a way to network and grow your reach and income.

You can keep this list on your website, in an Excel worksheet, or in a document. Update it as needed.

The way this is implemented in the podcast space is following an interview, asking the host or guest if they could provide an introduction for you to someone on your Dream 100 list if they are close with any of them, and then providing them your list.

This is how I got Mike Michalowicz on my show. He is another one I tried to get on, with no luck. But I was a guest on someone else's podcast who knew Mike, and he offered to put in a word for me with Mike and his team. It worked! The fact he was about to release a new book could've played a factor, as that is the best time to get a hard-to-get guest on your show. It was an example of the Dream 100 at play.

I will be including a Dream 100 reach spreadsheet in Podcast Profit Pro

Networking & Referrals

Similar to the Dream 100, networking and referrals are also an important part of your strategy to market and monetize your podcast. One of the biggest benefits I have found to have an interview-style podcast is the networking aspect. I have made so many powerful connections through podcast networking. And if you network enough, that could lead to referrals too. Maybe the person you are networking with that was a guest on your show or you were a guest on theirs, even if they don't need your product or service, perhaps someone they know might and they will refer you because they know you offer that product or service. Referrals and word-of-mouth marketing are still (and always will be) the number one way to accrue new customers, clients, and overall business.

Search Over Social

Yes, it is important to have a social media presence. It is also important to post on social media, like/comment on posts, and engage and interact with fans and customers. But, as we know, social feeds update quickly. Here today and gone tomorrow? More like here this second and gone the next.

Therefore, I recommend focusing more time and attention on platforms that operate more like search engines than that social media. There are several out there, but I want to touch on these three: YouTube, Pinterest, and Medium.

YouTube: YouTube is the second largest search engine in the world, following Google (who owns YouTube). People are always looking on YouTube for answers to their problems. So why not post your video podcast or take captioned social clips from the video podcast and create YouTube Shorts?

Pinterest: many people mis-classify Pinterest as a social media platform, when it is, in fact, a search engine. Similar to YouTube, people are looking for either answers on how to do something or looking for something to buy. What is different about this platform is its photo-based versus video-based like YouTube is. So you could create graphics for each episode (maybe even with quotes), linking back to the episode.

Medium: Medium is a platform where people can discover written content. It is a good place to post your blog-style show notes.

One big key to success on any of these platforms (and any online platform, period) is keywords and SEO.

Now, as far as social media goes, I would say one of the top platforms right now for discoverability is TikTok, like it or not. Also, Facebook Groups are great for engaging with people. It will go farther faster than just posting.

But if you don't want to spread yourself too thin and want to focus more on more evergreen platforms, I suggest using these searchable platforms.

Press, Publicity, and Reviews

There are a few ways to get free or affordable press and publicity, aside from being on podcasts. When you launch a new podcast, send out a press release with eReleases.

If you are an expert in your field and have a podcast about it, sign up for media/press alerts from HARO when someone is looking for a media piece in your area of expertise.

Apply for relevant speaking engagements, even if you have to do them for free. The exposure is worth it. If you don't feel comfortable speaking, then at least attend relevant conferences.

As mentioned in an earlier chapter, do free and affordable promotions or ads in various podcast directories and podcast player apps.

As also mentioned in an earlier chapter, do podcast swaps, drops, and rolls.

Look into promoting your podcast in relevant trade magazines, papers, or blogs.

Get more reviews and leverage that by social sharing. One way to do this is to offer a contest to your listeners where they enter a drawing to win something. They enter by leaving a review and subscribing/following your show. For social proof, they take a screenshot of their review, and they share that on social media and tag you. You could even offer to do review swaps.

A new resource that makes this easy and gamifies the process is PodLottery.

Make sure your podcast is distributed to all the podcast players and apps that you are aware of. I have a list available at Podcast Profit Pro.

III

MONETIZING A PODCAST

Book Funnel

Did you know that writing a book is one of the best ways to introduce potential customers to your brand and business? A book gives you instant credibility and clout in your subject. People will look at you and treat you differently once you can add *author* to your resume. Think of it as a glorified business card.

You may think it's out of the realm of possibility. But I believe we are all experts in something or have a unique story to tell, and others can enjoy our varied knowledge. It is now easier than ever to self-publish a book.

Most people don't even realize they have a book in them. Even if they do, they think they could never write it because they don't understand how to, are too scared to do so, feel they don't have the time, or a million other reasons.

Is there something that people have pointed out you're good at? Is there something you've researched? Is there something you've studied in depth or gone to school for? Whatever it is, we all have something we're an expert in whether or not we realize it. So why not share that with the world and make an impact all while making money off it, or building a brand and business around it?

Now, I know what you may be thinking: "Sarah, that sounds way too complicated, expensive, and time consuming. And who will publish my book?" You! That's right—you! We're in an interesting time now with the proliferation of self-publishing. There are a few companies who self-publish, but I use Kindle Direct Publishing (KDP) by Amazon. It's free to publish and you even get a free International Standard Book Number (ISBN) assigned. You don't have to order a bunch of books and store them. With no need to physically manage an inventory, there are no upfront expenses in that regard. Everything is printed on demand through Amazon KDP. Any time someone orders your book, Amazon prints it and ships it. It's that simple. Amazon = Amazing!

If you have a creative personality that likes to produce content, then writing a book would fulfill that creative itch. It's also original. Sure, there may be other books out there on your topic, but no one is coming at it from your unique angle and telling it the way only you can. It's always good to have a lot of different perspectives on the same topic. Why do we have so many fast-food burger joints, and why do they all seem to pop up on the same street corners as each other? There's room for many people in the same space, which is a good thing because it shows there's a market for it. So, don't let competition deter you. Another advantage is that a book is a good introduction to both you and your business. It's a glorified business card, if you will, and also creates instant credibility and authority in your niche.

A book as a business card is much more impressive than a standard business card, and it guarantees someone won't just toss it or forget about you. Most business cards end up in the trash, but a book won't. Even if the recipient never reads your book, they'll see it lying around, as will anyone else who comes to their house or office, or they'll give it away to someone who may be even more of your target customer than they were. Heck, maybe they'll even sell it to a bookstore or at a garage sale. Who cares? If it's in someone's hands, or on display somehow or some way, that's all that matters. Sure, this costs more than a business card, but regular business cards often get thrown away. To print a self-published book costs about $3 on average, give or take, depending on the number of pages.

Traditional Publishing vs. Self-Publishing

There is no right or wrong way to publish, but each method has its pros and cons. Unless you are a well-known authority figure or celebrity, it's difficult these days to get traditionally published. It usually requires you to complete your book and then pitch agents to sell your book to publishers. That can be a long, arduous process. And even if you get a publishing deal, it can still take many months—usually over a year—to get the book out on the market. If you want to get your book out quickly and on your terms and timing, then self-publishing is a better option.

The main benefits of being traditionally published are twofold: being in bookstores, and generally you'll receive an upfront bonus. But this isn't free money. All sales you make up to this amount count against your bonus. And then if you don't sell enough books, you have to pay back the difference. So, unless you know your book is going to sell, it may be disadvantageous to get an upfront bonus. Also, many people assume that having a traditional publishing deal means the publisher does all the marketing for you. From what I've been advised, this isn't the case. It's still the author's responsibility to take on most of the marketing. An advantage, depending on how you look at it, is that they take care of the costs of the cover, editing, etc. On the flip side, this may interfere with creative control.

The biggest advantage of self-publishing is that you are in complete control from start to finish. You control the timing, the creative aspects of the book, distribution channels, and everything else there is to publishing. In addition, a lot of self-published authors make more money than traditionally published authors because of a much higher earning percentage per book sold. You can list your book at any price you want and in general, Amazon takes 30% (e-book) or 40% (print). Whereas with traditionally published books, you usually make around $1 per book sold.

The only disadvantage of writing a book is that it takes time. It's one of the most time-consuming things you could do. But guess what? It may be a lot of work upfront but can provide a royalty check every month for years to come. The best part? Your copyright exists 70 years beyond your death. This means your children and grandchildren could earn monthly checks from your book(s). Talk about leaving a legacy!

Monetizing Your Book Beyond Book Sales

If you offer products and services beyond the book, then I advise to put a call to action in both the front and the back of your book. Heck, you can even intersperse it throughout the book. Just make sure it's not overkilled. A pleasant call to action offers something free (e.g., an audiobook version of the book, a downloadable cheat sheet, or an online course, etc.) in exchange for their email address so you can market your products and services to them later.

A great way to make the most out of your podcast appearances is to have a lead magnet or CTA of some sort. This could be as short and simple as a checklist, guide, roadmap, or something along those lines. However, I recommend writing and self-publishing a short book (such as this one) that shows off your expertise. The very idea of writing a book can sound overwhelming, but it doesn't have to be. I recommend writing a book right around 100 pages (just big enough to have a printable spine) such that a person can read it within an hour. The goal is so you can show just enough expertise to get someone to want to work with you. The goal isn't to sell books, but to give them away. Of course, you can also have it up for sale on Amazon, etc.

You can even hand this book out at relevant conferences that have your ideal customer. For example, I plan to pass this book out for free at podcast-specific conferences.

If you are a podcast host, having a book to give away is a good lead magnet or CTA, but it's especially useful for podcast guests. Think about it: you've already shared some of your expertise for 15-60+ minutes on a podcast episode. Listeners are just begging to learn more from you. You could even turn your book into an audiobook since we already know that podcast listeners are audio listeners.

If you want more information on self-publishing, I wrote a book on that topic (Authorpreneur), which is available on Amazon.

If you need hands-on help to get your book written and published, I recommend talking with Mike Capuzzi at Bite-Sized Books. We were guests on each other's podcasts. While I published all my books myself, I love the fact that he focuses on B2B and B2C short, helpful books (*Shooks*, as he calls them).

You can create a "free plus shipping" book funnel where you give your book away for free and just ask the customer to pay for the shipping/handling (which ends up still being cheaper than they could purchase the book for on Amazon). The effective thing about book funnels is you can have a bump offer, upsell, down sell, etc., on top of the fact you gather that potential client's email address for future marketing.

The software program I use and recommend for landing pages and sales funnels are Systeme.io. They even offer a free plan! I provide a "Free Book + Shipping" funnel that you can import for free into a free Systeme.io account at Podcast Profit Pro.

If you wish to create a funnel yourself or with your preferred software program, I created this funnel graphic below to give you a visual idea of how a book funnel can work for you:

27 WAYS TO MARKET AND MONETIZE A PODCAST

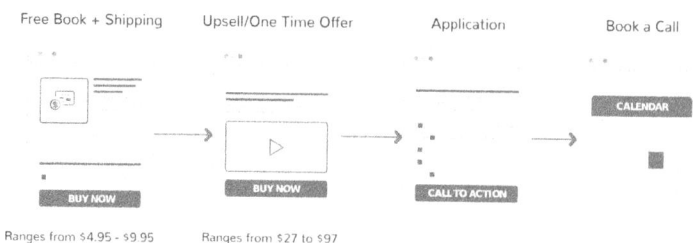

6 C's

The 6 C's:

- **Coaching**
- **Consulting**
- **Courses**
- **Community**
- **Crowdfunding**
- **Content Upgrades**

If you are a coach or consultant, having a podcast is a great way to display your expertise and get new customers and clients. There are a couple of ways to do this: listeners or guests. Listeners are having time to get to know, like, and trust you through your podcast, and may hire you as their coach or consultant at some point. A quicker option would be to have a coaching call and record it (get permission, of course) and release it as a podcast episode. This way your listeners are hearing how you process and handle issues, but also so the guest themselves experience firsthand how you can help them with their problems, and they may turn into a client.

If you don't wish to do one-on-one coaching or consulting, but have a lot of expertise in a particular subject, then creating a course is a great option. Instead of being one-on-one, this is one-to-many. It is also passive once you have recorded all your videos. It is learning-on-demand for your listeners and customers. Aside from coaching and consulting, offering a course is one of the most common ways to monetize a podcast. Of course, this isn't direct monetization as some other options, but in these cases, the podcast serves as the front end of your sales funnel.

Recommend Resource for Course Software: Systeme.io (they have a free plan). I have included a "free + shipping" share funnel inside Podcast Profit Pro.

If you like the idea of these, but don't feel comfortable charging the rates that coaching, consulting, and courses warrant, then just having a conversational community may work for you. This could serve the purpose of group coaching, or just to communicate with your listeners.

Another way to monetize a podcast is through crowdfunding or content upgrades. The way this works in the podcast world is that you provide some exclusive content such as behind-the-scenes, bonus episodes, private RSS feeds, podcast shoutouts, or merchandise to customers who pay you a monthly "membership" fee or a simple onetime donation. This usually ranges anywhere from $1 - $25 and beyond. They do this through a third-party site. I use and recommend PodInbox. Tip: you can have a section of your podcast involve listener questions and you can send your listeners to your PodInbox page to leave their voicemail that you can then download and splice into your podcast episodes. I have an extensive list inside Podcast Profit Pro.

3 M's

The 3 M's:

- **Memberships**
- **Masterminds**
- **Masterclasses**

Similar to coaching and consulting, memberships and masterminds are a good way to monetize a podcast. You could either record these calls and release them as podcast episodes, or create a membership or mastermind group on the back end as a CTA and listeners may join your program. Think of it more than group coaching with not just your input, but the input of several other people as well.

Membership can be like a community as well, but offers more than just a community factor and can offer classes/courses, spreadsheets, templates, and other assets. You can charge anywhere from $7 - $97 per month for a membership.

A mastermind is a much smaller group of people, usually only 20. Masterminds are much more expensive as well, ranging from $97 to $997 per month. Masterminds are filled with high-level learners and educators who want to do more than just communicate but grow their business.

A masterclass is like a webinar, with more teaching and less pitching. It lasts about an hour and the attendees walk away with some actionable steps taken. If you want to offer an online masterclass that ranges from 2 to 5 days, you could refer to it as a workshop, boot camp, or challenge. This involves a lot of learning, worksheets, and more. For masterclasses, workshops, boot camps, or challenges, these can range from free to $97.

Sponsorships

One of the most obvious, yet most difficult, ways to monetize a podcast is through the use of sponsorships.

There are a couple of problems with this method of monetization.

First, have thousands of downloads to even qualify for a sponsorship. In addition, a lot of sponsorships aren't targeted to your audience. There are a lot of podcasts out there with ads for mattresses, or meal delivery kits, but their podcast may be about entrepreneurship. What are the chances those listeners are going to check out those products or services? Not great.

You may view it as though you are getting paid regardless, so what difference should it make to you? Well, a lot. You don't want to do things that turn off your listeners. And I can tell you ads like that will.

If you are going to do sponsorships, I recommend they apply to your listeners first. Second, I recommend host-read ads which are where you are the one reading the ad in your voice versus some random person. It will be better received that way. It will seem less like a commercial, and one of the big reasons people listen to podcasts instead of the radio is they rarely have to deal with commercials. And if you do a host-read ad, I recommend easing it naturally into the content you are already discussing. Try to make it a part of your content if you can. I also recommend keeping the ad under thirty seconds and putting it in a mid-roll spot instead of a pre-roll. The reason being is that

I have found that if you have an ad (unless maybe it's for one of your products or services) right out of the gate; you are more likely to lose new listeners if an ad is a very first thing they hear at the beginning of each episode.

The only sponsorship platform I use and recommend is Podcorn. This is because it is the only one I am aware of that doesn't require podcasts to have a certain number of listeners or downloads to pitch or secure sponsorships. I will have an overview video of Podcorn at Podcast Profit Pro as well as a sponsorship spreadsheet template and sponsorship scripts.

Getting sponsors is a lot more work and more time-consuming than it is worth, especially if you are going with the CPM (cost per mille) method, which is roughly $25 per 1,000 downloads. The route I have taken and recommend is to approach relevant companies directly. Companies you either already use or recommend. Work out a flat-rate deal (either per episode or a block of episodes). This is what I have done, both inside and outside of Podcorn.

There are some podcasts where sponsorships make the most sense as their method of monetization. That would be super-niche (i.e., underwater basket weaving, because that's the go-to that everyone uses) or hyper-local (i.e., the city or town you live in). And with either of these types of podcasts, it is possible to secure sponsorships before you even launch the show.

I am in the beginning stages of planning my podcast for the town that I live in. I will do spotlight interviews with local businesses (restaurants, shops, etc). To monetize this type of show, I will offer and securing sponsored ads or featured spotlight episodes. When you are the only podcast in town (or on a certain subject like underwater basket weaving, for example), your buying power is increased because even if you only had 100 listeners, every single one of them is a potential customer.

In Podcast Profit Pro, I will break down how things go with my local podcast.

Affiliate Marketing

One of my favorite ways to monetize a podcast is through the use of affiliate marketing. Affiliate marketing is where you refer to a product or service you use and recommend. By using a special link provided to you by the company that offers the product or service, it then links back to you and you get paid a percentage or flat amount for any sales made through your unique link(s).

The product or service you are referring to would need to have an affiliate program for you to make a commission. Not that you shouldn't refer to products or services that don't have an affiliate program. I recommend products and services all the time that don't have an affiliate program. You should refer to products and services you use, recommend, know, like, and trust whether you'll make any money on the transaction.

You can look for relevant affiliate opportunities at an affiliate marketplace, but many products and services offer their in-house affiliate program that isn't a part of an affiliate marketplace. So, you can just go to the product or service website and search for the terms "affiliate" or "referral." It's usually in the footer, but if you can't find it, just search for it, and if you still can't find it, you can do a Google search for the "(product or service name) + affiliate." If you still find nothing, that likely shows they don't have an affiliate program, but you can always contact them and ask, and if they don't, you could express interest. Some companies implement an affiliate program just because someone said they wanted to promote that product or service. Worth a try.

Note: When promoting an affiliate offer always include a disclaimer stating that you make a commission on sales through your affiliate link, but then also assure your audience that you only recommend products or services you or someone you know has used and finds useful and relevant.

Pay to Play

Before I dive in here, let me first caveat with this: the pay-to-play method is a rare and potentially controversial way to make money podcasting. It is when a guest has to pay an "appearance fee" to be a guest on your show. This could range anywhere from under $100 all the way into the thousands of dollars.

While it is not a common practice at the time of this writing, it is becoming more common as the podcast industry grows. There are several big-name podcasters with big shows that charge thousands of dollars for a guest to have a 20 or 30 minute spot on their show. The thought process behind this is because if the guest has a particular book, product, service, program, etc that they want to get more publicity for and promote to a very niche podcast audience, it may be worth the "price of admission" so to speak. While the guest provides value to the audience during the interview, it also serves as almost a long-form commercial for them.

As a podcaster myself that loves to find new ways to market and monetize podcasts, I tested this out myself. A $50 appearance fee was what I started with. It quite surprised me at how many interested guests took me up on this offer. I felt I was on to something. But, almost just as many that were interested and willing, there were quite a few naysayers as well, because this isn't a common practice yet (if ever). I then raised the rate to $75 to test that price point, and while I got maybe a handful of guests interested, it seems $50 was the limit most guests felt they could justify for a show of my size.

My personal takeaway or lesson learned from this is that "pay-to-play" just isn't common enough to risk alienating and turning off potential good guests for a mere $50 (or whatever rate you determine). Perhaps someday this will become more common practice, and then one could re-evaluate the pros and cons, but it is not something I am doing again.

However, if this is something you are interested in, there is one resource I recommend which is Guestio. This platform is set up as "pay-to-play" so people coming on that platform to find podcasts to be on or guests to have on are acquainted with this concept. I will be including an overview video of this platform in Podcast Profit Pro.

For a deeper dive into this subject, here is a good Bloomberg article on this topic: PodSeam.com/payforplay.

If you don't want to do that, but still want to make money from podcast guests, consider the next option instead: Skip-The-Line.

Skip-The-Line

Skip-The-Line is like Pay-To-Play except that the guest only pays if they want their episode released on a certain date, week, or period. This is useful for guests who have a book, product, course, etc. coming out soon and don't want to wait weeks or months (depending on your backlog) for their episode to release.

It is especially common for authors to do podcast tours (think similar to a book tour back in the day). This is when an author will go on several podcasts in a short time right before a book launch to help increase awareness of their book and increase sales as well.

Podcast guests, especially those that would fall under the categories I mentioned, rarely frown upon being presented with this option. Keep in mind that the vast majority will decline the offer to skip the line because they maybe do not have a message, book, product, course, or service that is that time and therefore they don't care when their episode comes out. As long as it comes out eventually, of course.

Marketing Boost

A marketing boost is when you charge the guest a certain amount, but you use the vast majority of that money to boost their episode through paid social media ads. This is not something I have tried myself, but I have been on other shows that have offered this service. I declined it, which I regret now because I would have liked to see if or how much that would have increased the visibility of that podcast episode.

While this idea seems good in theory, it's not that great in reality. The bottom line is that most people on social media will not click over to listen to a podcast episode. That's not what they are on social media for. Sure, some may, but the vast majority won't. So, unless the podcast host is offering to boost your specific episode in podcast directory ads, it's not worth doing as a guest or offer as a host.

Guest to Client

Perhaps the most lucrative way to monetize a podcast is to have guests that might become future customers or clients of your products or services.

This requires some strategy because you wouldn't just have anyone on your show that fits your niche. It would be a very specific type of guest. One that you could see benefiting from your products or services.

You also need to be careful about how you approach this relationship. They don't want to be sold on the show or after the interview. You want to nurture that relationship. You may ask them if they'd be interested in joining your newsletter to receive future updates so that they will notice your offerings.

At a certain point, you could inquire if they've considered your services or working with you. It could take years (if ever) for any guest to become a customer or client of your products or services, so you don't want to go into the interview with that sole intention in mind. You want to give value to that person, too. But this is a valuable and viable strategy that could cause tens of thousands of dollars in new business, depending on your business model.

Conclusion

As succinct as this book is, I hope you found this information useful. If you are looking to expand your knowledge and dive deeper, be sure to check out these resources:

Get free access to some templates, resources, etc. mentioned in this book by going here:
PodcastProfitPro.com

Need help with your launching, managing, marketing, or monetizing your podcast?
See how we can help!
PodSeam.com

CONCLUSION

Scan the QR code below to listen to my podcast on your favorite listening device:

Also, if you found this book helpful and wouldn't mind doing so, please leave an honest rating and review wherever you purchased this book. It really helps a lot!

Thank you,
Sarah St John

About the Author

I am an entrepreneur, podcaster, author, animal lover, and world traveler. I've created several startups throughout my entrepreneurial career of over a decade. Through my books and podcast, my goal is to show you how to launch and manage an online business on a budget.

You can connect with me on:
- https://www.thesarahstjohn.com
- https://twitter.com/thesarahstjohn
- https://www.facebook.com/thesarahstjohn
- https://www.instagram.com/thesarahstjohn
- https://www.pinterest.com/frugalpreneur
- https://www.linkedin.com/in/sarah-stjohn
- https://www.youtube.com/channel/UCFWxBqAsNhV4K8iR3UQ2_IA
- https://podseam.com
- https://podcastresourcedirectory.com

Subscribe to my newsletter:

✉ https://sendfox.com/sarahstjohn

Also by Sarah St John

Frugalpreneur: How To Launch, Manage and Market Your Online Business For Under $100 Per Month (Preneur Series Book 1)

Authorpreneur: How to Self Publish and Launch a Book to Build Your Business (Preneur Series Book 2)

Podcastpreneur: How to Produce, Promote, and Profit With A Podcast (Preneur Series Book 3)

www.ingramcontent.com/pod-product-compliance
Lightning Source LLC
Chambersburg PA
CBHW070311220526
45465CB00004B/1838